Junior Ranger

by Samuel Malkin
illustrated by Marcelo Elizalde

Harcourt
SCHOOL PUBLISHERS

Cover, ©George H. H. Huey/CORBIS; p.6–7, ©Bill Ross/CORBIS; p.8, ©Corbis; p.9, ©Robert Campbell/SuperStock; p.11, ©NATIONAL PARK SERVICE; p.12, ©Corbis/PunchStock; p.13, ©James Urbach/SuperStock.

Printed in China

ISBN 10: 0-15-350189-8
ISBN 13: 978-0-15-350189-0

Ordering Options
ISBN 10: 0-15-349939-7 (Grade 4 ELL Collection)
ISBN 13: 978-0-15-349939-5 (Grade 4 ELL Collection)
ISBN 10: 0-15-357280-9 (package of 5)
ISBN 13: 978-0-15-357280-7 (package of 5)

1 2 3 4 5 6 7 8 9 10 985 12 11 10 09 08 07 06

My name is Jose Morales. Bryce Canyon National Park is one of my favorite places in the world. Bryce Canyon National Park is located in the state of Utah. It was named after a pioneer farmer named Ebenezer Bryce. Mr. Bryce moved to this land in the 1870s. He helped build roads through the canyons. People started to call the place Bryce Canyon while he still lived there. The land became a national park in 1928.

I want to be a park ranger here when I grow up. Park rangers take care of parks like Bryce Canyon. Rangers study and protect plants and animals in the park. Rangers also protect the park from fires.

Park rangers also teach visitors about Bryce Canyon National Park. Rangers take visitors on tours of the park. Rangers also help young people like me. I am a Junior Park Ranger. Let me tell you all about it!

If you want to become a Junior Ranger at Bryce Canyon, you must do the following things:

- Meet with a park ranger to learn about the park.
- Complete the pages in an activity book.
- Collect and throw away a bag of litter.

Litter is trash, and it is important to throw away trash to keep the park nice and clean. The park ranger told us that most people are very careful about throwing away their trash. I did find some trash on a hiking trail, so I picked it up.

There are more than 300 national parks in the United States. Land that is in a national park is protected by the government. No one can build on the land or destroy it. The wildlife that lives there is protected, too. People can enjoy these parks forever.

Bryce Canyon National Park is one of the smallest national parks in the United States, but it is still a big place! More than one million people visit Bryce Canyon National Park every year. There are many wonderful things to see.

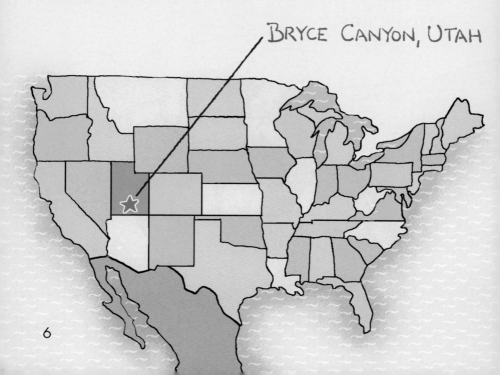

BRYCE CANYON, UTAH

Most visitors come to see the huge rocks. These rocks were made millions of years ago. Earthquakes and volcanoes made the earth shift. As the earth moved, canyons formed. A canyon is the space between two mountains or two cliffs. Canyons often have water flowing through them. Canyons have high, steep sides.

Wind, rain, and ice carved the rocks in the park into interesting shapes. Bryce Canyon National Park is filled with "hoodoos." A hoodoo is a tall, skinny rock. A hoodoo looks like an upside-down icicle. Some hoodoos are as tall as a human being. Some hoodoos are taller than a building that has ten floors!

Wind, rain, and ice also made this rock
bridge in the park. The weather still pounds
through the rocks in Bryce Canyon National
Park. The weather slowly carves new shapes
out of the rocks.

My family met Park Ranger Karen Jones when we visited the park. She reminded us that it is important to carry a bottle of water and to use sunscreen when hiking in the park. Then she told us about some of the interesting things to see in the park.

For example, Ranger Jones told us that there are many kinds of pine trees in the park. There are Ponderosa pine trees in Ponderosa Canyon. Some Ponderosa pines are five feet (1.52 m) wide. I am almost five feet tall! Some pine trees are 150 feet (45 m) tall.

Ranger Jones told us about an area of the park called Rainbow Point. You can see rocks in a rainbow of colors when you stand at Rainbow Point. Ranger Jones said that these rocks are called Pink Cliffs, Gray Cliffs, White Cliffs, Vermilion (bright red) Cliffs, and Chocolate Cliffs. These are pretty names for a very beautiful place!

Pronghorm antelope

Ranger Jones also told us about the wildlife in the park. There are many animals, including mountain lions. Mountain lions are also called cougars and pumas. Pronghorn antelopes, snakes, and lizards also live in the park.

It is fun to look for Utah prairie dogs in the park. They are not really dogs but are relatives of squirrels. Utah prairie dogs dig holes and tunnels under the ground. They live together in large groups called "prairie dog towns." The prairie dogs hibernate under the ground during the winter. In March, they wake up and come out of their underground homes.

Osprey

As Ranger Jones talked, she suddenly looked up. She pointed to the sky. An osprey flew high above us. Everybody stood still. The large brown and white bird landed in a nest in a tall tree.

Ranger Jones told us there are many other birds in the park. The birds that live in Bryce Canyon include the California condor and the violet-green swallow. This bird actually is violet, or purple, and green!

I wanted to become a Junior Ranger more than ever after I saw the natural wonders in Bryce Canyon National Park. I completed the pages in the activity book. I picked up litter from one of the trails. Then I took the Junior Ranger pledge. A pledge is a kind of promise.

As a Junior Ranger I promised to help protect the plants and animals in Bryce Canyon National Park. I also promised to keep on learning about the natural world. I am proud to be a Junior Ranger. I plan to become a park ranger when I grow up. I will always protect and learn about the natural world.

Scaffolded Language Development

ADJECTIVES Review adjectives with students by pointing out examples in the book, such as *large* and *interesting*. Then review the adjectives in the word bank with students by reading each word and giving an example of something that each could describe, such as *a tall tree* and *a pink pig*. Then have students chorally complete the sentences with words from the word bank.

Word Bank: tall, skinny, interesting, pink, gray, red

1. The osprey flew up high and then landed in a _____ tree.
2. A hoodoo is a long, _____ rock.
3. _____, _____, and _____ are some of the colors in Rainbow Point.
4. The rocks have _____ shapes.

 Science

Nature Study Have students page through the book and choose an animal or a natural wonder that particularly interests them. Then help students find out more about it. Ask students to write a list of words that describes their choice.

School-Home Connection

Favorite Scenery Have students talk to family members about the most beautiful natural area they have ever seen. Have them ask what animals, plants, or rocks were there? What was the weather like?

Word Count: 914 (917)